THE DANDIE DINMONT TERRIER

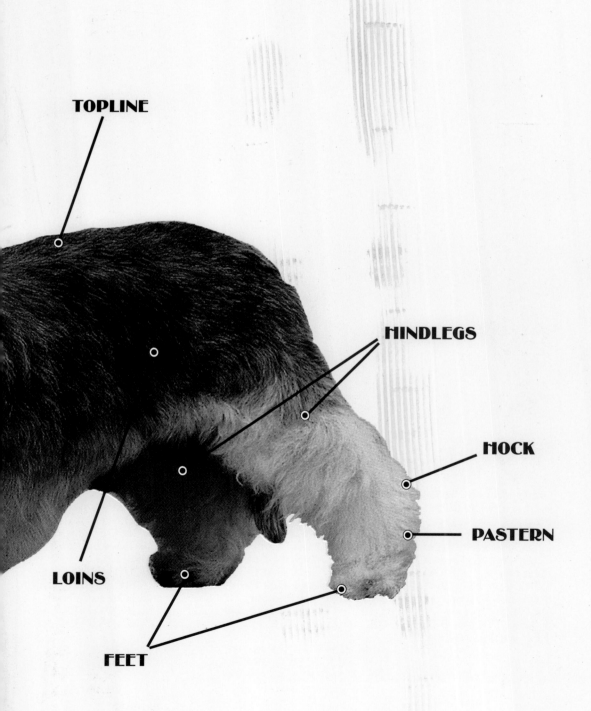

TOPLINE

HINDLEGS

HOCK

PASTERN

LOINS

FEET

Title Page: Dandie Dinmont photographed by Isabelle Francais.

Photographers: Isabelle Francais, Booth Photography, Tara Darling.

Distributed in the UNITED STATES to the Pet Trade by T.F.H. Publications, Inc., One T.F.H. Plaza, Neptune City, NJ 07753; distributed in the UNITED STATES to the Bookstore and Library Trade by National Book Network, Inc. 4720 Boston Way, Lanham MD 20706; in CANADA to the Pet Trade by H & L Pet Supplies Inc., 27 Kingston Crescent, Kitchener, Ontario N2B 2T6; Rolf C. Hagen Inc., 3225 Sartelon St. Laurent-Montreal Quebec H4R 1E8; in CANADA to the Book Trade by Vanwell Publishing Ltd., 1 Northrup Crescent, St. Catharines, Ontario L2M 6P5 ; in ENGLAND by T.F.H. Publications, PO Box 15, Waterlooville PO7 6BQ; in AUSTRALIA AND THE SOUTH PACIFIC by T.F.H. (Australia), Pty. Ltd., Box 149, Brookvale 2100 N.S.W., Australia; in NEW ZEALAND by Brooklands Aquarium Ltd. 5 McGiven Drive, New Plymouth, RD1 New Zealand; in Japan by T.F.H. Publications, Japan—Jiro Tsuda, 10-12-3 Ohjidai, Sakura, Chiba 285, Japan; in SOUTH AFRICA by Lopis (Pty) Ltd., P.O. Box 39127, Booysens, 2016, Johannesburg, South Africa. Published by T.F.H. Publications, Inc.

MANUFACTURED IN THE
UNITED STATES OF AMERICA
BY T.F.H. PUBLICATIONS, INC.

DANDIE DINMONT TERRIER

A COMPLETE AND RELIABLE HANDBOOK

by Mrs. William M. Kirby

RX-122

CONTENTS

DESCRIPTION OF THE DANDIE DINMONT TERRIER

There are few breeds that can match the "bonny" charm of the Dandie Dinmont Terrier. These Dandie puppies have that characteristic sparkle in their eyes!

Out of the mists of the Cheviot Hills in the border country between England and Scotland has come the "bonny terrier"—the Dandie Dinmont. He is a rascal that will look up at you with mischievous eyes in a cherubic face and win your heart for all time.

The Dandie is one of the beloved breeds of the British Isles, and we are constantly meeting these pepper (gray) or mustard (tan) terriers in English novels. From the time Auld Pepper, Auld Mustard, Young Pepper, and Young Mustard romped through the pages of Sir Walter Scott's *Guy Mannering* to more recent times when we find a Dandie defen-

sively guarding Fleur Forsythe Mont's baby in the opening pages of John Galsworthy's *The Silver Spoon*, the Dandie Dinmont has been a part of English and Scottish life.

The breed has become increasingly popular in America. More and more frequently you see the short-legged little fellow being walked on the street, head held high and tail swinging leisurely; you catch a glimpse of an enchanting face with dark, luminous eyes under a silky topknot looking with

The Dandie has a long history as one the most beloved working breeds of England and Scotland.

interest and animation from a car window; or you will see him playing with a group of children, as happily intent upon their game and as much a part of it as if he were himself a child.

Wherever he is known he is adored, for he has a charm and a fascination about him that is his alone. Besides his quaint appearance, his wisdom, his pluck, his courage, and his watchfulness, what endears him most to all who know him is his responsiveness. If you are tired of the indifference of certain breeds, you will be charmed with the warmth of the Dandie's nature and his constant awareness of you. Whenever you speak to him, there comes the eager answering slap of his expressive tail, showing he is ready at all times to do what you want him to do. When you know him, only his loyalty to you will exceed your loyalty to him.

The Dandie's expression has typical terrier "pluck" coupled with an awareness of the world around him. King's Mtn. Pixie Montizard owned by Julie and Doug Young.

DESCRIPTION

APPEARANCE

Quite different in appearance from the more familiar terrier breeds with their straight lines, the Dandie is made up of curves. The Dandie's head is large, but not out of proportion to the body, and full-domed, with a topknot of soft, silky, silvery or cream-colored hair that covers the entire head but does not hide the eyes. The eyes are round, fairly

prominent, set wide apart, and of a rich dark hazel color, giving the face a wide-awake, alert, intelligent expression. The ears are pendant, set rather low on the head; they carry a "tassel" or fringe of hair the color of the topknot on the tip. The muzzle is strong, the jaw powerful and punishing, and the teeth should meet in a "scissors bite." The neck is strong and muscular. The forelegs are short and well boned, with strong paws for digging; the hind legs are longer but not so heavy, causing one dog columnist to write facetiously, "This later enables it

The Dandie Dinmont is a long-bodied breed whose small size allows him to exist in any environment.

to walk uphill while remaining on a level keel at all times, but since the leg combination is awkward for downhill runs, the Dandies eventually become concentrated on hilltops." The body is long and flexible with a deep, powerful chest and well-sprung ribs. The topline is lower just behind the shoulders, gracefully arching up over the loins and then sloping gently down to the root of the tail. The tail is short, about 8 to 10 inches long, and rather thick at the root, tapering to a point and carried gaily with a scimitar-like curve above the level of the back.

These puppies represent the pepper and mustard color variations found in the Dandie Dinmont.

The Dandie comes in two colors—pepper and mustard. The pepper includes all shades from a bluish-black to a silvery gray. The mustards vary

from a rich red gold to a pale fawn, with the brilliant mustard color the more desirable. The body coats of both are a mixture of hard and soft hair— approximately twice as much soft as hard—giving a crisp but not wiry feeling to the hand. The hair on the underbody is of a softer texture and lighter in color. The muzzle is covered with hair a little darker than the topknot and of the same texture as the

DESCRIPTION

feathering on the forelegs. The Dandie's height is 8 to 11 inches at the shoulder, and his weight is between 18 and 24 pounds. He is a real dog, but one small enough to fit in anywhere.

PERSONALITY

The Dandie was bred originally as a companion and a working terrier, going to ground for badger, woodchuck, and sometimes fox. In America he is bred as a companion, a watchdog, and a fun dog to live with, but if he ever encounters a rat or a mouse, the old hunting instinct comes to the fore and the varmint is dispatched forthwith. Because of his charming personality, his quiet dignity, and his unusual amount of good sense, he is unexcelled as a family dog. With his own he is gay and fun loving, responsive and affectionate; with strangers he is polite but indifferent; and above all he likes to make

Although originally bred as a working terrier, today's Dandie is known largely as a companion dog and family member. Julie Young with three eight-week-old puppies.

his own advances. The "come here, little doggie" bit is not for him, but in his own good time, if left alone, he will come close, nuzzle an outstretched hand, and indicate that he is ready to be friends. He makes an ideal playmate for children and an understanding companion for grownups, as no dog is more loyal to his human family or more protective should the occasion demand. He is always ready for a romp or a rough-house, but he will lie quietly if a small youngster wants to use him as a soft warm pillow at nap time.

It is preferable to breed one color of Dandie to the other. This ensures a brightly colored coat of the proper texture. Owner, France Roozen.

COLOR

A breeder of Dandies should have both peppers and mustards, as one color complements the other. If one has seen only the adult dogs, the first litter may be quite a surprise, as the pepper puppies look like black satin with mustard trim on their faces and feet. Gradually, as the hair gets longer, more and more silver comes to the coat, making it a penciled gray. At one year of age, the topknot will have "cleared"—becoming silky and curly and pure silver in color. The mustard puppies will have a dark overlay of hair and will look for all the world like red squirrels. This overlay is the puppy coat and will all comb and brush out by the time the puppies are four or five months old, leaving their body coats bright mustard, and at a year of age they will have full creamy topknots. The more the puppies are combed, the more colorful the adult coats will be.

It is not mandatory, but the preferred way to breed is to mate one color with the other. If two peppers are mated, the resulting puppies will all be peppers, but if this is continued through several generations, there will be a loss of the desired mustard trim on the face and feet, the topknots will be "smoky" (fail to clear), and the coats will tend to be too soft. If two mustards are mated, most of the puppies will be mustards, though a few peppers may appear. Continued mustard-to-mustard mating, however, can result in coats that are too pale, and the bright mustard body coat is greatly to be desired. In pepper-to-mustard mating, all of the puppies may be one color or the other, but as a rule some are peppers and some mustards, with the peppers generally predominating. This method of mating not only keeps the colors going strong and true but also helps in maintaining the proper texture of coat.

As for the Dandie puppies—with their big, round inquiring eyes and their infinite capacity for fun and frolic—they are irresistible.

DANDIES AT DOG SHOWS

The exemplary behavior of Dandies at benched shows is always cause for comment, as their section is so very quiet. There is never any barking or lunging at passersby. The dogs sit quietly, surveying the "goings on," responding happily to any attention given them, often clowning a bit, and are all eagerness and joy when their owners appear to take them to exercise or to the show ring. In the ring, the Dandie has been termed the "gentleman of the terrier group." Others may growl and snarl and strain on their leashes to get at other dogs, but the Dandie stands, interested and attentive, with tail gently waving. Should an attack be made upon him, however, his fighting spirit would be aroused and his low growl would sound a warning. He will never look for or start trouble, he will only react to any aggressive behavior toward him.

Opposite: Dandie Dinmonts are known for their grace and exemplary behavior and are often termed "the gentlemen of the terrier group."

DANDIE DINMONT HISTORY

Originating somewhere along the Scottish border, these terriers early in the 18th century were famed throughout the countryside for their indomitable courage in the extermination of foxes, badgers, and other vermin and were used extensively to run with packs of Otterhounds along the river banks. In all probability they are the descendants of those hardy dogs owned by the traveling gypsies and tinkers who wandered through the Cheviot Hills between England and Scotland. The earliest records tell of William, or "Piper," Allan, who was born in 1704. Though he was a tinker by trade, Will was a great hunter and seems to have spent much of his time pursuing the otter and playing the bagpipes. He always kept a dozen or more sporting terriers, his most outstanding one being a dog named Charley. One day, after a hunting expedition, Lord Ravensworth, through his agent, tried to buy the dog, but Will answered without hesitation, "By the wuns, his hale estate canna buy Charley." Another of Will's favorites was a dog named Peachem, about whom he said, "When Peachem goes mouth, I durst sell the otter's skin."

It was not until 1814, when Sir Walter Scott published his novel *Guy Mannering,* his well known tale of the border country, that these dogs became known elsewhere. In 1885, Charles Cook, writing the first authoritative history of the Dandie, wrote as follows: "It seems that Sir Walter, while sojourning in the borders, when Sheriff of Selkirkshire, had heard of the renown of the various 'store farmers' and shepherds and their terriers as hunters of the fox and otter in the hills and dales of the then wild border country, and with his usual facility, when writing *Guy Mannering* he wrote into his romance, the charming character of Dandie Dinmont, the burly tenant of Charlieshope with his inimitable race of terriers, 'Auld Pepper' and 'Auld Mustard,'

Opposite: The Dandie Dinmont Terrier's reputation originated in Scotland and in England where he was valued as a hunting and companion dog.

'Young Pepper' and 'Young Mustard' and 'Little Pepper' and 'Little Mustard.' Sir Walter wrote of them, 'they fear nothing that ever cam' wi' a hairy skin on't.'"

This character of Dandie Dinmont had a counterpart in real life, James Davidson of Hindlee, in the County of Roxburgh, who was a great hunter and whose breed of terriers was the best in the country. There seems little reason to doubt that these were the same race and blood as the dogs that belonged to the Allans and their neighbors, for originally Davidson procured these terriers from Holystone on Coquet Water, the native heath of the Allans. Following the publication of *Guy Mannering* these dogs came to public attention and were much sought after, being called at first Dandie Dinmont's Terriers. Later the possessive was dropped and they were known as Dandie Dinmont Terriers. Had Sir Walter Scott not written *Guy Mannering*, the breed might never have been given this name.

Since the time of James Davidson the breed has been carefully preserved and little change has occurred throughout the years. Modern breeding has not altered

Throughout the centuries the Dandie's characteristics have been carefully preserved and his original type and conformation retained.

The Dandie Dinmont derives his name from a character in a book by Sir Walter Scott, who praised the terrier's fearlessness and personality.

the original type; the present-day Dandie possesses to a remarkable degree the conformation and characteristics of the 18th-century terrier. He is still the same wise, self-possessed, dignified, affectionate companion almost human in his understanding and sympathy, with the same grit and courage as his forebears. Sir Walter and his Dandie had their portrait painted by Landseer, as did the Duke of Buccleuch by Gainsborough, the dogs looking much as they do today. The two Dandies portrayed in a famous painting by Arthur Wardle done in 1897 could do well in today's show ring. The Dandie Dinmont was first recognized and shown in England in the 1860s, and the first club was founded in 1875.

BRIEF HISTORY OF DANDIES IN AMERICA

In 1886 three Dandies were imported from Scotland by Mr. and Mrs. John Naylor of Chicago and registered in the American Kennel Club stud book. From 1908 to 1928 Mr. Alfred B. Maclay (Killearn Kennels) was actively showing. Around 1928 the R. Stockton Whites and their daughter, Mrs. Lawrence Illoway (Buccleuch Kennels), and Mrs. Richard H. Johnston (Ruffcote Kennels) started showing consistently and were active in founding the Dandie Dinmont Terrier Club of America, which held its first meeting in 1932. In 1933 the Overhill Kennels took up Dandies, buying breeding stock from the Ruffcote Kennels, and this established bloodline has been maintained to the present day. There was little activity through the war years, but in 1947 Miss Sarah Swift (Cliffield Kennels) imported Ch. Flornell Beetham Skittle and later Ch. Waterbeck Watermark from Mr. George Jardine, owner of the famous Waterbeck Kennels in Scotland. Since then, Cliffield built up an outstanding show record and Watermark has many champions to his credit. Other breeders are coming to the fore across the country and it is good to see the Dandie being appreciated in an ever-widening circle. We who have the future of the breed at heart, however, agree with John F. Gordon when he writes of the Dandie that "In public esteem he is highly held by those who breed and love him, but there are still many rungs in the ladder to be climbed to general popularity, and although there is plenty of room in the land for the Dandie to introduce himself, it will be a sorry day for him and his admirers should he achieve the excessive popularity of those dogs who have suffered excessive commercialism and an undoubted ruination of correct type and temperament."

Having a high order of intelligence and a great willingness to please, Dandies do well in obedience work, and they get along well with other household pets and with other dogs.

DANDIES WITH THEATER PEOPLE

The Robert Montgomerys bought their first Dandie puppy, Overhill Ringleader, in 1952. Later they acquired a female from Cliffield, campaigned her to her championship, bred her to Ch. Waterbeck Watermark, and raised a litter. Out of this litter came Ch. Swan Cover Highland Hercules, who retired with 109 Best of Breed wins and 22 Group placements, and was himself the sire of champions, including the 1964 Westminster BOB Ch. Topnotch Alacazam; and the 1963 National Specialty Winner, Ch. Ceolaire Bannockburn. Paul Lynde had a pepper male, Overhill Harry, who made fast friends for the breed wherever he went. Paul said that his friends said of their dogs, "I am going to keep Rex—or Roscoe—or Rufus—as long as he lives, but when he goes, I want one just like Harry."

When the national company of *My Fair Lady* was being cast in New York, one of the members, Robert Driscoll, came to the Westminster show and fell in love with the Dandies. Later he bought a pepper female, named her Overhill My Fair Lady, and for the next five years she traveled with the company from one end of the United States to the other, returning to her home kennel for only the ten weeks when the company took the show to Russia.

The Dandie's accommodating personality and high intelligence win him loyal friends wherever he goes!

OFFICIAL STANDARD FOR THE DANDIE DINMONT TERRIER

For those who fancy the Dandie Dinmont Terrier, the standard of the breed is a vital tool in breeding the ideal dog. A standard is a written description of this "ideal dog," a dog that in actuality has never existed and never will. The following standard is the approved standard of the American Kennel Club, the principal governing body for the dog sport in the United States. The standard is drafted and proposed by the national parent club, and then accepted by AKC. As the parent club sees fit, the standard can change from time to time, though these changes are essentially quite minor, usually pertaining to the format of the standard itself or perhaps some word choice. Studying the breed standard will reveal much about the dog itself, its character, and its ideal physique. Whether you are interested in breeding, showing, or just enjoying your dog, the standard makes required reading for any breed fancier.

General Appearance—Originally bred to go to ground, the Dandie Dinmont Terrier is a long, low-stationed working terrier with a curved outline. The distinctive head with silken topknot is large but in proportion to the size of the dog. The dark eyes are large and round with a soft, wise expression. The sturdy, flexible body and scimitar shaped tail are covered with a rather crisp double coat, either mustard or pepper in color.

Size, Proportion, Substance—*Height* is from 8 to 11 inches at the top of the shoulders. *Length* from top of shoulders to root of tail is one to two inches less than twice the height. For a dog in good working condition, the preferred **weight** is from 18 to 24 pounds. Sturdily built with ample bone and well developed muscle, but without coarseness. The overall balance is more important than any single specification.

Head—The *head* is strongly made and large, but in proportion to the dog's size. Muscles are well developed, especially those covering the foreface. The **expression** shows great determination, intelligence and dignity. The **eyes** are large, round, bright and full, but not protruding. They are set wide apart and low, and directly forward. Color, a rich dark hazel.

A breed standard is a set of traits that ideal representatives of the breed should possess. Montizard's Toot-A-Loo owned and bred by Julie and Doug Young.

A Dandie's head should be large but proportionate to the dog's body, and his eyes should be full, dark and round.

Eye rims dark. The **ears** are set well back, wide apart and low on the skull, hanging close to the cheek, with a very slight projection at the fold. The shape is broad at the base, coming almost to a point. The front edge comes almost straight down from base to tip; the tapering is primarily on the back edge. The cartilage and skin of the ear are rather thin. The ear's length is from three to four inches.

The **skull** is broad between the ears, gradually tapering toward the eyes, and measures about the same from stop to occiput as it does from ear to ear. Forehead (brow) well domed. Stop well defined. The *cheeks* gradually taper from the ears toward the muzzle in the same proportion as the taper of the skull. The *muzzle* is deep and strong. In length, the proportions are a ratio of three (muzzle) to five (skull). The nose is moderately large and black or dark colored. The lips and inside of the mouth are black or dark colored. The teeth meet in a tight scissors bite. The *teeth* are very strong, especially the canines, which are an extraordinary size for a small dog. The canines mesh well with each other to give great

The Dandie Dinmont's body is long and low to the ground, consisting of a flat level topline and a tail that stands erect and tapers to a point.

holding and punishing power. The incisors in each jaw are evenly spaced and six in number.

Neck, Topline, Body—The *neck* is very muscular, well developed and strong, showing great power of resistance. It is well set into the shoulders and moderate in length. The *topline* is rather low at the shoulder, having a slight downward curve and a corresponding arch over the loins, with a very slight gradual drop from the top of the loins to the root of the tail. Both sides of the backbone well muscled. The outline is a continuous flow from the crest of the neck to the tip of the tail. The *body* is long, strong and flexible. *Ribs* are well sprung and well rounded. The *chest* is well developed and well let down between the forelegs.

The underline reflects the curves of the topline. The *tail* is 8 to 10 inches in length, rather thick at the root, getting thicker for about four inches, then tapering off to a point. The set-on of the tail is a continuation of the very slight gradual drop over the croup. The tail is carried a little above the level of the body in a curve like a scimitar. Only when the dog is excited may the tip of the tail be aligned perpendicular to its root.

Forequarters—There should be sufficient layback of *shoulder* to allow good reach in front; angulation in balance with hindquarters. *Upper arms* nearly equal in length to the shoulder blades, elbows lying close to

The body coat of the Dandie Dinmont is a mixture of $^2/_3$ hardish hair with $^1/_3$ soft hair giving it a sort of crisp texture.

the ribs and capable of moving freely. The **forelegs** are short with good muscular development and ample bone, set wide apart. Feet point forward or very slightly outward. Pasterns nearly straight when viewed from the side. Bandy legs and fiddle front are objectionable.

Hindquarters—The **hind legs** are a little longer than the forelegs and are set rather wide apart, but not spread out in an unnatural manner. The upper and lower thighs are rounded and muscular and approximately the same length; stifles angulated, in balance with forequarters. The hocks are well let down and rear pasterns perpendicular to the ground.

Feet—The *feet* are round and well cushioned. Dewclaws preferably removed on forelegs. Rear feet are much smaller than the front feet and have no dewclaws. Nails strong and dark; nail color may vary according to the color of the dog. White nails are permissible. Flat feet are objectionable.

Coat—This is a very important point: The hair should be about two inches long; the body coat is a mixture of about 2/3 hardish hair with about 1/3 soft hair, giving a sort of crisp texture. The hard is not wiry. The body coat is shortened by plucking. The coat is termed pily or pencilled, the effect of the natural intermingling of the two types of hair. The hair on the underpart of the body is softer than on the top.

The Dandie Dinmont's head is covered by a silky coat that extends to a distinctive topknot that covers the upper portion of the ears and frames the eyes.

STANDARD

The head is covered with very soft, silky hair, the silkier the better. It should not be confined to a mere topknot but extends to cover the upper portion of the ears, including the fold, and frames the eyes. Starting about two inches from the tip, the ear has a thin feather of hair of nearly the same color and texture as the topknot, giving the ear the appearance of ending in a distinct point. The body of the ear is covered with short, soft, velvety hair. The hair on the muzzle is of the same texture as the foreleg feather. For presentation, the hair on the top of the muzzle is shortened. The hair behind the nose is naturally more sparse for about an inch.

The forelegs have a feather about two inches long, the same texture as the muzzle. The hind leg hair is of the same texture but has considerably less feather. The upper side of the tail is covered with crisper hair than that on the body. The underside has a softer feather about two inches long, gradually shorter as it nears the tip, shaped like a scimitar. Trimming for presentation is to appear entirely natural; exaggerated styling is objectionable.

Color—The color is pepper or mustard.

Pepper ranges from dark bluish black to a light silvery gray, the intermediate shades preferred. The

According to the breed standard, the Dandie Dinmont should be one of two colors: pepper, which ranges from a bluish-black to a slivery gray; and mustard, which varies from reddish brown to pale fawn.

The overall appearance and temperament of the Dandie Dinmont is one of independence and intelligence, combined with an affectionate nature.

topknot and ear feather are silvery white, the lighter the color the better. The hair on the legs and feet should be tan, varying according to the body color from a rich tan to a very pale fawn.

Mustard varies from a reddish brown to a pale fawn. The topknot and ear feather are a creamy white. The hair on the legs and feet should be a darker shade than the topknot.

In both colors the body color comes well down the shoulders and hips, gradually merging into the leg color. Hair on the underpart of the body is lighter in color than on the top. The hair on the muzzle (beard) is a little darker shade than the topknot. Ear color harmonizes with the body color. The upper side of the tail is a darker shade than the body color, while the underside of the tail is lighter, as the legs. Some white hair on the chest is common.

Gait—Proper movement requires a free and easy stride, reaching forward with the front legs and driving with evident force from the rear. The legs move in a straight plane from shoulder to pad and hip to pad. A stiff, stilted, hopping or weaving gait and lack of drive in the rear quarters are faults to be penalized.

Temperament—Independent, determined, reserved and intelligent. The Dandie Dinmont Terrier combines an affectionate and dignified nature with, in a working situation, tenacity and boldness.

Approved February 9, 1991
Effective March 27, 1991

BREED REQUIREMENTS

ENVIRONMENT

The Dandie seems happy and well adjusted in any type of home. In the country he will spend his days outdoors, accompanying members of his family at their work or the children in their play or just going about his own business of investigating whatever claims his interest, coming in at night tired and content to lie at someone's feet through the evening.

In the city, a fenced yard in which to play is quite adequate—somewhere where he can chase a ball, carry sticks, or just race wildly in his exuberance and joy of living and then climb on lawn furniture to rest. No dog should be allowed to roam the city streets. This can only court disaster in one form or another.

As long as the Dandie Dinmont has a place to get comfortable, he is happy in all types of home environments.

If the Dandie is to be an apartment dweller, this will suit him just fine, but he must be taken out at regular intervals for his duties, and it will please him very much if at least one outing a day consists of a brisk walk of several blocks. Here paper-training is a great convenience in bad weather and for the times when he must be left alone for longer than usual. Take him out with you whenever possible. A walk delights him—the longer the better. He is always eager to go in the car and, if you can take him on vacation trips, he will be little trouble and add much to your pleasure.

The sturdiness of his heritage allows the Dandie to thrive in any climate. He delights in outdoor activities and is always eager to play.

BREED REQUIREMENTS

GEOGRAPHICAL LIMITATIONS

It doesn't seem to matter in the least to a Dandie where he goes to live. The sturdiness of his heritage stands him in good stead, and he seems to adjust to any climatic conditions. I know of two in Stick, Alaska, that swam in the Sound, worried the animals they came across in the woods, and once frightened off a bear with the commotion they made on discovering him.

A pair went to Cuernavaca, Mexico, to a news correspondent and his wife, where they played havoc with the formal garden and had to be restrained from playing in the fountain. The gentleman was rebased in Europe and the family made its home in Palermo, Sicily; the Dandies, of course, went along.

A doctor from Ohio retired and took his family and his pepper Dandie puppy to live in their vacation home on St. Croix in the Virgin Islands. There Rhett, as he was called, went on the family's sailboat, swam in the Caribbean, and kept the property free of hermit crabs. At night, when he heard one rattling across the patio, there was a lot of barking because he couldn't get out to chase it away.

Happy Dandies, like these eight-month-old pups, are welcomed anywhere they go!

GROOMING YOUR DANDIE DINMONT

COMBING, BRUSHING, AND TRIMMING

Every Dandie owner should invest in a metal terrier comb, nail clippers, a pair of scissors, a good dog brush, and a dog dresser or some other stripping tool such as a stripping comb. With this equipment the dog can be kept in good condition at home without professional help. Dandies do not shed, but daily combing is essential, especially in the first year so that the soft puppy coat never becomes matted and so that combing is always a pleasant

Regular grooming will have your dog looking just "Dandie" in no time!

experience, which it will not be for either you or the puppy if the hair becomes tangled. It takes only a few minutes when done every day, and the better the puppy is combed and brushed, the more colorful its adult coat will be. When the adult coat is in, daily combing takes out any loose hair, allowing new hair to start growing in, which keeps the coat "rolling," as we say. Then if the nails are clipped occasionally; the hair trimmed off the top of the muzzle (a path as wide as the black part of the nose up to the stop and even with the eyes); the edges of the ear trimmed down to the fringe; the hair cut around the feet to make them look round and neat, and under the tail, for sanitary reasons; and the wispy shaggy ends of the topknot nipped off with the stripping comb, the home Dandie will look well groomed and cared for.

Opposite: Grooming for the show ring is an involved procedure; the idea is to pay detailed attention to the coat and accentuate the dog's strong points.

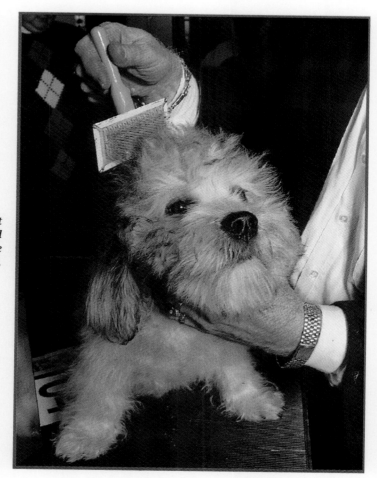

Your Dandie's topknot should be brushed up and any shaggy ends should be trimmed.

When grooming your Dandie's hair in front of the collar line, trim the hair off the top of the muzzle to the stop, making a path as wide as his nose.

Grooming for the show ring is somewhat different, for the idea here is to present the dog with detailed attention to coat and outline of body and to accentuate his good points and perhaps improve upon points where he is deficient, all of which can be done by subtle trimming.

Three to four months before the date of a show, the body coat should be pulled off with thumb and forefinger or with a dull stripping tool, thus allowing a new two-inch show coat to grow in by show time. Put the dog on a table and comb him well. Then tie an imaginary line around his neck, pushing it well up behind the ears. Comb all hair in front of this line forward. Then, behind the line, pluck out all old hair on the neck down to the chest in front, on the sides of the neck down over the shoulders to the elbows, on the back and sides down to a line running from the elbows to three inches or so below the set on of tail, and under the tail behind. Take off all hair on the tail. Comb all long hair on the chest, underbody, quarters, hocks, and front legs, and carefully pluck by hand all hairs that are shaggy and spoil the appearance, watching for outline as each hair is pulled out. On the front legs, comb the hair up and shorten it on the sides so that when the dog is in motion he does not look out at the elbows. Clean off the inside of the hocks to give the rear a neat appearance. Cut the nails and trim the hair around the edges of the feet and between the pads with scissors.

What is done with the hair in front of the collar line on a Dandie Dinmont is the most important part of his grooming; the part that makes him look distinc-

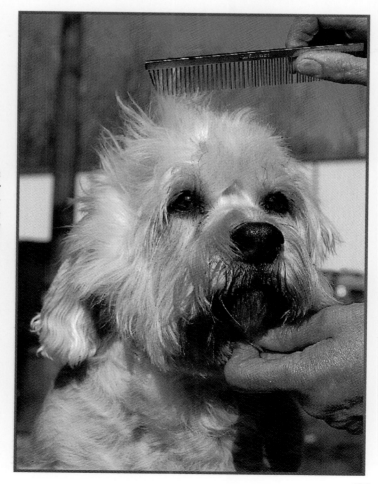

Pay special attention when grooming around your Dandie's head and face; this is the area that gives him his eye-catching and distinctive look.

tive and different; the part that gives him captivating, eye-catching appeal. In the rough, he may look a bit "witchy," but properly groomed he is definitely "bewitching."

First with the scissors, trimming tool, or finger and thumb, take the hair off the top of the muzzle up to the stop (just beyond the inside corner of the eye), making a path as wide as the black part of his nose. Now go to the ears. *Do not take the hair off the entire ear* from where it joins the skull, but note where the ear folds over. Push back all hair above the fold into the topknot (this adds to the width of head) and clean off the ear part of the way down, leaving the long hair on the tip as a fringe. Cut hair off the inside of the ear down to the fringe. Trim the edges of the ear, on the back from where the ear joins the skull. On the front, form a tuft that is pushed back into the topknot, down to the fringe.

Now for the topknot, the Dandie's most distinctive point. Comb whiskers and all hair on the head forward. After selecting your trimming tool, turn back the ear and hold the whiskers in your left hand. *Do not clean off the cheek* but with careful strokes shorten the hair in front of the ears down to even with the eyes, leaving it at least an inch and a half long and blending it carefully into the length of the whiskers. Comb the topknot again and shape from front to back and from side to side, taking off all wispy, shaggy ends, making the whole head look as large and round as possible. The joy of this is that the more the ragged ends are nipped off, the more beautifully full the topknot grows, so that it does not need "starching" but stays up at all times, making a light background for the dark, luminous eyes and giving the Dandie his attractive, appealing appearance. An exaggerated topknot spoils the balance of the dog and is generally left to cover some fault.

Three weeks before the show, the long eyelashes and the hair around the eyes—more below than above—is pulled out with thumb and index finger, as the dark lid and the new black hair that comes in tend to enhance the depth and beauty of the eyes. At this time, too, shorten the hair on neck and shoulders, blending carefully into the show coat, and give attention again to the nose, ears, feet, and furnishings. Bathe the dog if necessary to have him immaculate, but do it several days prior to the show so as not to soften the crispness of his coat.

BATHING

When a Dandie is given daily attention with comb and brush he seldom needs a bath. Certainly it need not be a weekly custom. Bathe him only when you feel it is necessary or when he is definitely dirty. Use a good dog shampoo, be sure he is rinsed well, and towel him dry. Then keep him inside and warm for several hours after the bath. With puppies, I like to dry them, wrap them in a fresh dry towel and then in a woolen blanket, and hold them, letting their body heat keep them cozy and warm until I am sure there is no chance of chilling.

A well-groomed Dandie can really go places in conformation showing. Ch. Attieson Of Erlwood owned by David Ruml and I.F. Zimmerman being awarded a Group First by Anna Katherine Nicholas.

YOUR PUPPY'S NEW HOME

Before actually collecting your puppy, it is better that you purchase the basic items you will need in advance of the pup's arrival date. This allows you more opportunity to shop around and ensure you have exactly what you want rather than having to buy lesser quality in a hurry.

It is always better to collect the puppy as early in the day as possible. In most instances this will mean that the puppy has a few hours with your family before it is time to retire for his first night's sleep away from his former home.

Your new puppy will need special attention when you bring him home, so make sure you have all the basic equipment you need ready for his arrival.

If your puppy is going on a long car trip, a crate will provide him with a safe place to sleep or lie down.

If the breeder is local, then you may not need any form of box to place the puppy in when you bring him home. A member of the family can hold the pup in his lap—duly protected by some towels just in case the puppy becomes car sick! Be sure to advise the breeder at what time you hope to arrive for the puppy, as this will obviously influence the feeding of the pup that morning or afternoon. If you arrive early in the day, then they will likely only give the pup a light breakfast so as to reduce the risk of travel sickness.

41

PUPPY'S NEW HOME

If the trip will be of a few hours duration, you should take a travel crate with you. The crate will provide your pup with a safe place to lie down and rest during the trip. During the trip, the puppy will no doubt wish to relieve his bowels, so you will have to make a few stops. On a long journey you may need a rest yourself, and can take the opportunity to let the puppy get some fresh air. However, do not let the puppy walk where there may have been a lot of other dogs because he might pick up an infection. Also, if he relieves his bowels at such a time, do not just leave the feces where they were dropped. This is the height of irresponsibility. It has resulted in many public parks and other places actually banning dogs. You can purchase poop-scoops from your pet shop and should have them with you whenever you are taking the dog out where he might foul a public place.

Your journey home should be made as quickly as possible. If it is a hot day, be sure the car interior is

On his car ride to his new home, stop and let your puppy outside for fresh air and to relieve himself often.

amply supplied with fresh air. It should never be too hot or too cold for the puppy. The pup must never be placed where he might be subject to a draft. If the journey requires an overnight stop at a motel, be aware that other guests will not appreciate a puppy crying half the night. You must regard the puppy as a baby and comfort him so he does not cry for long periods. The worst thing you can do is to shout at or smack him. This will mean your relationship is off to a really bad start. You wouldn't smack a baby, and your puppy is still very much just this.

Upon his arrival, your Dandie puppy should be given a comfortable place to rest and relax. This is Ch. Dunsdale Dinita, CD at 12 weeks old owned by France Roozen.

ON ARRIVING HOME

By the time you arrive home the puppy may be very tired, in which case he should be taken to his sleeping area and allowed to rest. Children should not be allowed to interfere with the pup when he is sleeping. If the pup is not tired, he can be allowed to investigate his new home—but always under your close supervision. After a short look around, the puppy will no doubt appreciate a light meal and a drink of water. Do not overfeed him at his first

Puppies love to chew on things, so make sure that all electrical appliances are neatly hidden from view and unplugged when not in use.

meal because he will be in an excited state and more likely to be sick.

Although it is an obvious temptation, you should not invite friends and neighbors around to see the new arrival until he has had at least 48 hours in which to settle down. Indeed, if you can delay this longer then do so, especially if the puppy is not fully vaccinated. At the very least, the visitors might introduce some local bacteria on their clothing that the puppy is not immune to. This aspect is always a risk when a pup has been moved some distance, so the fewer people the pup meets in the first week or so the better.

DANGERS IN THE HOME

Your home holds many potential dangers for a little mischievous puppy, so you must think about these in advance and be sure he is protected from them. The more obvious are as follows:

Open Fires. All open fires should be protected by a mesh screen guard so there is no danger of the pup being burned by spitting pieces of coal or wood.

Electrical Wires. Puppies just love chewing on things, so be sure that all electrical appliances are neatly hidden from view and are not left plugged in when not in use. It is not sufficient simply to turn the plug switch to the off position—pull the plug from the socket.

Open Doors. A door would seem a pretty innocuous object, yet with a strong draft it could kill or injure a puppy easily if it is slammed shut. Always ensure there is no risk of this happening. It is most likely during warm weather when you have windows or outside doors open and a sudden gust of wind blows through.

Balconies. If you live in a high-rise building, obviously the pup must be protected from falling. Be sure he cannot get through any railings on your patio, balcony, or deck.

Be especially cautious with your puppies around the holidays, when things like lights and small ornaments can be a hazard.

Ponds and Pools. A garden pond or a swimming pool is a very dangerous place for a little puppy to be near. Be sure it is well screened so there is no risk of the pup falling in. It takes barely a minute for a pup—or a child—to drown.

The Kitchen. While many puppies will be kept in the kitchen, at least while they are toddlers and not able to control their bowel movements, this is a room full of danger—especially while you are cooking. When cooking, keep the puppy in a play pen or in another room where he is safely out of harm's way. Alternatively, if you have a carry box or crate, put him in this so he can still see you but is well protected.

Be aware, when using washing machines, that more than one puppy has clambered in and decided to have a nap and received a wash instead! If you leave the washing machine door open and leave the room for any reason, then be sure to check inside the machine before you close the door and switch on.

Small Children. Toddlers and small children should never be left unsupervised with puppies. In spite of such advice it is amazing just how many people not only do this but also allow children to pull and maul pups. They should be taught from the outset that a puppy is not a plaything to be dragged about the home—and they should be promptly scolded if they disobey.

Children must be shown how to lift a puppy so it is safe. Failure by you to correctly educate your children about dogs could one day result in their getting a very nasty bite or scratch. When a puppy is lifted, his weight must always be supported. To lift the pup, first place your right hand under his chest. Next, secure the pup by using your left hand to hold his neck. Now you can lift him and bring him close to your chest. Never lift a pup by his ears and, while he can be lifted by the scruff of his neck where the fur is loose, there is no reason ever to do this, so don't.

Beyond the dangers already cited you may be able to think of other ones that are specific to your home—steep basement steps or the like. Go around your home and check out all potential problems—you'll be glad you did.

THE FIRST NIGHT

The first few nights a puppy spends away from his mother and littermates are quite traumatic for him. He will feel very lonely, maybe cold, and will certainly miss the heartbeat of his siblings when sleeping. To help overcome his loneliness it may help to place a clock next to his bed—one with a loud tick. This will in some way soothe him, as the clock ticks to a rhythm not dissimilar from a heart beat. A cuddly toy may also help in the first few weeks. A dim nightlight may provide some comfort to the puppy, because his eyes will not yet be fully able to see in the dark. The puppy may want to leave his bed for a drink or to relieve himself.

If the pup does whimper in the night, there are two things you should not do. One is to get up and chastise him, because he will not understand why you are shouting at him; and the other is to rush to comfort him every time he cries because he will quickly realize that if he wants you to come running all he needs to do is to holler loud enough!

A cuddly toy may help your puppy adjust to being in his new home. Ch. Montizard Calligraphy owned by Doug and Julie Young.

By all means give your puppy some extra attention on his first night, but after this quickly refrain from so doing. The pup will cry for a while but then settle down and go to sleep. Some pups are, of course, worse than others in this respect, so you must use balanced judgment in the matter. Many owners take their pups

to bed with them, and there is certainly nothing wrong with this.

The pup will be no trouble in such cases. However, you should only do this if you intend to let this be a permanent arrangement, otherwise it is hardly fair to the puppy. If you have decided to have two puppies, then they will keep each other company and you will have few problems.

OTHER PETS

If you have other pets in the home then the puppy must be introduced to them under careful supervision. Puppies will get on just fine with any other pets—but you must make due allowance for the respective sizes of the pets concerned, and appreciate that your puppy has a rather playful nature. It would be very foolish to leave him with a young rabbit. The pup will want to play and might bite the bunny and get altogether too rough with it. Kittens are more able to defend themselves from overly cheeky pups, who will get a quick scratch if they overstep the mark. The adult cat could obviously give the pup a very bad scratch, though generally cats will jump clear of pups and watch them from a suitable vantage point. Even-

If you housetrain your dog properly as a puppy, he will always know where to go to eliminate.

tually they will meet at ground level where the cat will quickly hiss and box a puppy's ears. The pup will soon learn to respect an adult cat; thereafter they will probably develop into great friends as the pup matures into an adult dog.

HOUSETRAINING

Undoubtedly, the first form of training your puppy will undergo is in respect to his toilet habits. To achieve this you can use either newspaper, or a large litter tray filled with soil or lined with newspaper. A puppy cannot control his bowels until he is a few months old, and not fully until he is an adult. Therefore you must anticipate his needs and be prepared for a few accidents. The prime times a pup will urinate and defecate are shortly after he wakes up from a sleep, shortly after he has eaten, and after he has been playing awhile. He will usually whimper and start searching the

Give your puppy lots of safe chew toys to encourage constructive chewing.

room for a suitable place. You must quickly pick him up and place him on the newspaper or in the litter tray. Hold him in position gently but firmly. He might jump out of the box without doing anything on the first one or two occasions, but if you simply repeat the procedure every time you think he wants to relieve himself then eventually he will get the message.

When he does defecate as required, give him plenty of praise, telling him what a good puppy he is. The litter tray or newspaper must, of course, be cleaned or replaced after each use—puppies do not like using a dirty toilet any more than you do. The pup's toilet can be placed near the kitchen door and as he gets older the tray can be placed outside while the door is open. The pup will then start to use it while he is outside. From that time on, it is easy to get the pup to use a given area of the yard.

Many breeders recommend the popular alternative of crate training. Upon bringing the pup home, introduce him to his crate. The open wire crate is the best choice, placed in a restricted, draft-free area of the home. Put the pup's Nylabone® and other favorite toys in the crate along with a wool blanket or other suitable bedding. The puppy's natural cleanliness instincts prohibit him from soiling in the place where he sleeps, his crate. The puppy should be allowed to go in and out of the open crate during the day, but he should sleep in the crate at the night and at other intervals during the day. Whenever the pup is taken out of his crate, he should be brought outside (or to his newspapers) to do his business. Never use the crate as a place of punishment. You will see how quickly your pup takes to his crate, considering it as his own safe haven from the big world around him.

THE EARLY DAYS

You will no doubt be given much advice on how to bring up your puppy. This will come from dog-owning friends, neighbors, and through articles and books you may read on the subject. Some of the advice will be sound, some will be nothing short of rubbish. What you should do above all else is to keep an open mind and let common sense prevail over prejudice and worn-out ideas that have been handed down over the centuries. There is no one way that is superior to all others, no more than there is no one dog that is exactly a replica of another. Each is an individual and must always be regarded as such.

A dog never becomes disobedient, unruly, or a menace to society without the full consent of his owner. Your puppy may have many limitations, but the singular biggest limitation he is confronted with in so many instances is his owner's inability to understand his needs and how to cope with them.

IDENTIFICATION

It is a sad reflection on our society that the number of dogs and cats stolen every year runs into many thousands. To these can be added the number that get lost. If you do not want your cherished pet to be lost or stolen, then you should see that he is carrying a permanent identification number, as well as a temporary tag on his collar.

Permanent markings come in the form of tattoos placed either inside the pup's ear flap, or on the inner side of a pup's upper rear leg. The number given is then recorded with one of the national registration companies. Research laboratories will not purchase dogs carrying numbers as they realize these are clearly someone's pet, and not abandoned animals.

Your small puppy is very vulnerable to outside dangers. It is up to you, his owner, to keep him as safe and secure as possible.

As a result, thieves will normally abandon dogs so marked and this at least gives the dog a chance to be taken to the police or the dog pound, when the number can be traced and the dog reunited with its family. The only problem with this method at this time is that there are a number of registration bodies, so it is not always apparent which one the dog is registered with (as you provide the actual number). However, each registration body is aware of his competitors and will normally be happy to supply their addresses. Those holding the dog can check out which one you are with. It is not a perfect system, but until such is developed it's the best available.

Make sure your Dandie Dinmont wears a collar and tags at all times in case he ever gets lost.

A temporary tag takes the form of a metal or plastic disk large enough for you to place the dog's name and your phone number on it—maybe even your address as well. In virtually all places you will be required to obtain a license for your puppy. This may not become applicable until the pup is six months old, but it might apply regardless of his age. Much depends upon the state within a country, or the country itself, so check with your veterinarian if the breeder has not already advised you on this.

FEEDING YOUR DANDIE DINMONT

Dog owners today are fortunate in that they live in an age when considerable cash has been invested in the study of canine nutritional requirements. This means dog food manufacturers are very concerned about ensuring that their foods are of the best quality. The result of all of their studies, apart from the food itself, is that dog owners are bombarded with advertisements telling them why they must purchase a given brand. The number of products available to you is unlimited, so it is hardly surprising to find that dogs in general suffer from obesity and an excess of vitamins, rather than the reverse. Be sure to feed age-appropriate food—puppy food up to one year of age, adult food thereafter. Generally breeders recommend dry food supplemented by canned, if needed.

Your puppy receives his nutrition from his mother when first born, but you, the owner, will be responsible for his diet once you bring him home. Owners, Julie and Doug Young.

FACTORS AFFECTING NUTRITIONAL NEEDS

Activity Level. A dog that lives in a country environ-

ment and is able to exercise for long periods of the day will need more food than the same breed of dog living in an apartment and given little exercise.

Quality of the Food. Obviously the quality of food will affect the quantity required by a puppy. If the nutritional content of a food is low then the puppy will need more of it than if a better quality food was fed.

Balance of Nutrients and Vitamins. Feeding a puppy the correct balance of nutrients is not easy because the average person is not able to measure out ratios of one to another, so it is a case of trying to see that nothing is in excess. However, only tests, or your veterinarian, can be the source of reliable advice.

Genetic and Biological Variation. Apart from all of the other considerations, it should be remembered that each puppy is an individual. His genetic make-up will influence not only his physical characteristics but also his metabolic efficiency. This being so, two pups from the same litter can vary quite a bit in the amount of food they need to perform the same function under the same conditions. If you consider the potential combinations of all of these factors then you will see that pups of a given breed could vary quite a bit in the amount of food they will need. Before discussing feeding quantities it is valuable to know at least a little about the composition of food and its role in the body.

COMPOSITION AND ROLE OF FOOD

The main ingredients of food are protein, fats, and carbohydrates, each of which is needed in relatively large quantities when compared to the other needs of vitamins and minerals. The other vital ingredient of food is, of course, water. Although all foods obviously contain some of the basic ingredients needed for an animal to survive, they do not all contain the ingredients in the needed ratios or type. For example, there are many forms of protein, just as there are many types of carbohydrates. Both of these compounds are found in meat and in vegetable matter—but not all of those that are needed will be in one particular meat or vegetable. Plants, especially, do not contain certain amino acids that are required for the synthesis of certain proteins needed by dogs.

Likewise, vitamins are found in meats and vegetable matter, but vegetables are a richer source of most. Meat contains very little carbohydrates. Some vitamins can be synthesized by the dog, so do not need to be supplied via the food. Dogs are carnivores and this means their digestive tract has evolved to need a high quantity of meat as compared to humans. The digestive system of carnivores is unable to break down the tough cellulose walls of plant matter, but it is easily able to assimilate proteins from meat.

In order to gain its needed vegetable matter in a form that it can cope with, the carnivore eats all of its prey. This includes the partly digested food within the stomach. In commercially prepared foods, the cellulose is broken down by cooking. During this process the vitamin content is either greatly reduced or lost altogether. The manufacturer therefore adds vitamins once the heat process has been completed. This is why commercial foods are so useful as part of a feeding regimen, providing they are of good quality and from a company that has prepared the foods very carefully.

Proteins

These are made from amino acids, of which at least ten are essential if a puppy is to maintain healthy growth. Proteins provide the building blocks for the puppy's body. The richest sources are meat, fish and poultry, together with their by-products. The latter will include milk, cheese, yogurt, fishmeal,

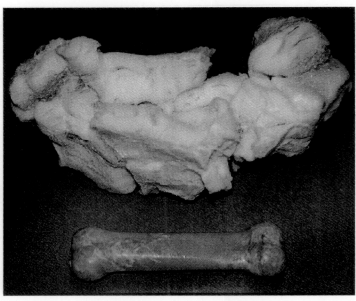

POPpups™ are 100% edible and enhanced with dog-friendly ingredients like liver, cheese, spinach, carrots or potatoes. They contain no salt, sugar, alcohol, plastic or preservatives. You can even microwave a POPpup™ to turn into a huge crackly treat.

and eggs. Vegetable matter that has a high protein content includes soy beans, together with numerous corn and other plant extracts that have been dehydrated. The actual protein content needed in the diet will be determined both by the activity level of the dog and his age. The total protein need will also be influenced by the digestibility factor of the food given.

Fats

These serve numerous roles in the puppy's body. They provide insulation against the cold, and help buffer the organs from knocks and general activity shocks. They provide the richest source of energy, and reserves of this, and they are vital in the transport of vitamins and other nutrients, via the blood, to all other organs. Finally, it is the fat content within a diet that gives it palatability. It is important that the fat content of a diet should not be excessive. This is because the high energy content of fats (more than twice that of protein or carbohydrate) will increase the overall energy content of the diet. The puppy will adjust its food intake to that of its energy needs, which are obviously more easily met in a high-energy diet. This will mean that while the fats are providing the energy needs of the puppy, the overall diet may not be providing its protein, vitamin, and mineral needs, so signs of protein deficiency will become apparent. Rich sources of fats are meat, their byproducts (butter, milk), and vegetable oils, such as safflower, olive, corn or soy bean.

Roar-Hide® is completely edible and is high in protein (over 86%) and low in fat (less than one-third of 1%). Unlike common rawhide, it is safer, less messy and more fun.

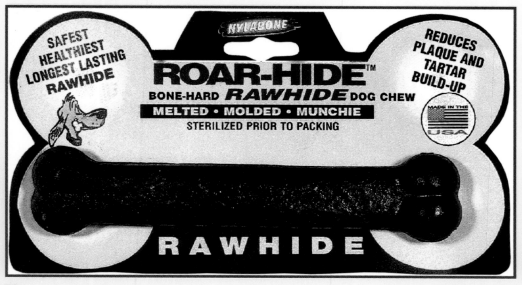

Carrots are rich in fiber, carbohydrates and vitamin A. The CarrotBone™ by Nylabone® is a durable chew containing no plastics or artificial ingredients and it can be served as-is, in a bone-hard form, or microwaved to a biscuity consistency.

Carbohydrates

These are the principal energy compounds given to puppies and adult dogs. Their inclusion within most commercial brand dog foods is for cost, rather than dietary needs. These compounds are more commonly known as sugars, and they are seen in simple or complex compounds of carbon, hydrogen, and oxygen. One of the simple sugars is called glucose, and it is vital to many metabolic processes. When large chains of glucose are created, they form compound sugars. One of these is called glycogen, and it is found in the cells of animals. Another, called starch, is the material that is found in the cells of plants.

Vitamins

These are not foods as such but chemical compounds that assist in all aspects of an animal's life. They help in so many ways that to attempt to describe these effectively would require a chapter in itself. Fruits are a rich source of vitamins, as is the liver of most animals. Many vitamins are unstable and easily destroyed by light, heat, moisture, or rancidity. An excess of vitamins, especially A and D, has been proven to be very harmful. Provided a puppy is receiving a balanced diet, it is most unlikely there will be a deficiency, whereas hypervitaminosis (an excess of vitamins) has become quite common due to owners and breeders feeding unneeded supplements. The only time you should feed extra vitamins to your puppy is if your veterinarian advises you to.

Minerals

These provide strength to bone and cell tissue, as well as assist in many metabolic processes. Examples are calcium, phosphorous, copper, iron, magnesium, selenium, potassium, zinc, and sodium. The recommended amounts of all minerals in the diet has not been fully established. Calcium and phosphorous are known to be important, especially to puppies. They help in forming strong bone. As with vitamins, a mineral deficiency is most unlikely in pups given a good and varied diet. Again, an excess can create problems—this applying equally to calcium.

Water

This is the most important of all nutrients, as is easily shown by the fact that the adult dog is made up of about 60 percent water, the puppy containing an even higher percentage. Dogs must retain a water balance, which means that the total intake should be balanced by the total output. The intake comes either by direct input (the tap or its equivalent), plus water released when food is oxidized, known as metabolic water (remember that all foods contain the elements hydrogen and oxygen that recombine in the body to create water). A dog without adequate water will lose condition more rapidly than one depleted of food, a fact common to most animal species.

AMOUNT TO FEED

The best way to determine dietary requirements is by observing the puppy's general health and physical appearance. If he is well covered with flesh, shows good bone development and muscle, and is an active alert puppy, then his diet is fine. A puppy will consume about twice as much as an adult (of the same breed). You should ask the breeder of your puppy to show you the amounts fed to their pups and this will be a good starting point.

The puppy should eat his meal in about five to seven minutes. Any leftover food can be discarded or placed into the refrigerator until the next meal (but be sure it is thawed fully if your fridge is very cold).

If the puppy quickly devours its meal and is clearly still hungry, then you are not giving him enough food. If he eats readily but then begins to

Make sure your Dandie has cool, clean water available to him at all times.

pick at it, or walks away leaving a quantity, then you are probably giving him too much food. Adjust this at the next meal and you will quickly begin to appreciate what the correct amount is. If, over a number of weeks, the pup starts to look fat, then he is obviously overeating; the reverse is true if he starts to look thin compared with others of the same breed.

WHEN TO FEED

It really does not matter what times of the day the puppy is fed, as long as he receives the needed quantity of food. Puppies from 8 weeks to 12 or 16 weeks need 3 or 4 meals a day. Older puppies and adult dogs should be fed twice a day. What is most important is that the feeding times are reasonably regular. They can be tailored to fit in with your own timetable—for example, 7 a.m. and 6 p.m. The dog will then expect his meals at these times each day. Keeping regular feeding times and feeding set amounts will help you monitor your puppy's or dog's health. If a dog that's normally enthusiastic about mealtimes and eats readily suddenly shows a lack of interest in food, you'll know something's not right.

TRAINING YOUR DANDIE DINMONT TERRIER

Once your puppy has settled into your home and responds to his name, then you can begin his basic training. Before giving advice on how you should go about doing this, two important points should be made. You should train the puppy in isolation of any potential distractions, and you should keep all lessons very short. It is essential that you have the full attention of your puppy. This is not possible if there are other people about, or televisions and radios on, or other pets in the vicinity. Even when the pup has become a young adult, the maximum time you should allocate to a lesson is about 20 minutes. However, you can give the puppy more than one lesson a day, three being as many as are recommended, each well spaced apart.

Before beginning a lesson, always play a little game with the puppy so he is in an active state of mind and thus more receptive to the matter at hand. Likewise, always end a lesson with fun-time for the pup, and always—this is most important—end on a high note, praising the puppy. Let the lesson end when the pup has done as you require so he receives lots of fuss. This will really build his confidence.

COLLAR AND LEASH TRAINING

Training a puppy to his collar and leash is very easy. Place a collar on the puppy and, although he will initially try to bite at it, he will soon forget it, the more so if you play with him. You can leave the collar on for a few hours. Some people leave their dogs' collars on all of the time, others only when they are taking the dog out. If it is to be left on, purchase a narrow or round one so it does not mark the fur.

Once the puppy ignores his collar, then you can attach the leash to it and let the puppy pull this along behind it for a few minutes. However, if the pup starts to chew at the leash, simply hold the leash but keep it slack and let the pup go where he wants. The idea is to let him get the feel of the leash, but not get in the habit of chewing it. Repeat this a couple of times a day for two days and the pup will get used to the leash without thinking that it will restrain him—which you will not have attempted to do yet.

Next, you can let the pup understand that the leash will restrict his movements. The first time he realizes this, he will pull and buck or just sit down. Immediately call the pup to you and give him lots of fuss. Never tug on the leash so the puppy is dragged along the floor, as this simply implants a negative thought in his mind.

Training your Dandie Dinmont to wear his leash and collar is important for his safety. Owner, France Roozen.

TRAINING

THE COME COMMAND

Come is the most vital of all commands and especially so for the independently minded dog. To teach the puppy to come, let him reach the end of a long lead, then give the command and his name, gently pulling him toward you at the same time. As soon as he associates the word come with the action of moving toward you, pull only when he does not respond immediately. As he starts to come, move back to make him learn that he must come from a distance as well as when he is close to you. Soon you may be able to practice without a leash, but if he is slow to come or notably disobedient, go to him and pull him toward you, repeating the command. Never scold a dog during this exercise—or any other exercise. Remember the trick is that the puppy must want to come to you. For the very independent dog, hand signals may work better than verbal commands.

THE SIT COMMAND

As with most basic commands, your puppy will learn this one in just a few lessons. You can give the puppy two lessons a day on the sit command but he will make just as much progress with one 15-minute lesson each day. Some trainers will advise you that you should not proceed to other commands until the

Training your eager-to-please Dandie Dinmont to obey basic commands is easy. With practice, persistence and patience, you'll have a well-trained companion in no time!

Ch. Dunsandle Jiminy demonstrates his puppy "sit." Owner, France Roozen.

previous one has been learned really well. However, a bright young pup is quite capable of handling more than one command per lesson, and certainly per day. Indeed, as time progresses, you will be going through each command as a matter of routine before a new one is attempted. This is so the puppy always starts, as well as ends, a lesson on a high note, having successfully completed something.

Call the puppy to you and fuss over him. Place one hand on his hindquarters and the other under his upper chest. Say "Sit" in a pleasant (never harsh) voice. At the same time, push down his rear end and push up under his chest. Now lavish praise on the puppy. Repeat this a few times and your pet will get the idea. Once the puppy is in the sit position you will release your hands. At first he will tend to get up, so immediately repeat the exercise. The lesson will end when the pup is in the sit position. When the puppy understands the command, and does it right away, you can slowly move backwards so that you are a few feet away from him. If he attempts to come to you, simply place him back in the original position and start again. Do not attempt to keep the pup in the sit position for too long. At this age, even a few seconds is a long while and you do not want him to get bored with lessons before he has even begun them.

TRAINING

THE HEEL COMMAND

All dogs should be able to walk nicely on a leash without their owners being involved in a tug-of-war. The heel command will follow leash training. Heel training is best done where you have a wall to one side of you. This will restrict the puppy's lateral movements, so you only have to contend with forward and backward situations. A fence is an alternative, or you can do the lesson in the garage. Again, it is better to do the lesson in private, not on a public sidewalk where there will be many distractions.

With a puppy, there will be no need to use a choke collar as you can be just as effective with a regular one. The leash should be of good length, certainly not too short. You can adjust the space between you, the puppy, and the wall so your pet has only a small amount of room to move sideways. This being so, he will either hang back or pull ahead—the latter is the more desirable state as it indicates a bold pup who is not frightened of you.

Hold the leash in your right hand and pass it through your left. As the puppy moves ahead and strains on the leash, give the leash a quick jerk backwards with your left hand, at the same time saying "Heel." The position you want the pup to be in is such that his chest is level with, or just behind, an imaginary line from your knee. When the puppy is in this position, praise him and begin walking again, and the whole exercise will be repeated. Once the puppy begins to get the message, you can use your left hand to pat the side of your knee so the pup is encouraged to keep close to your side.

It is useful to suddenly do an about-turn when the pup understands the basics. The puppy will now be behind you, so you can pat your knee and say "Heel." As soon as the pup is in the correct position, give him lots of praise. The puppy will now be beginning to associate certain words with certain actions. Whenever he is not in the heel position he will experience displeasure as you jerk the leash, but when he comes alongside you he will receive praise. Given these two options, he will always prefer the latter—assuming he has no other reason to fear you, which would then create a dilemma in his mind.

Once the lesson has been well learned, then you can adjust your pace from a slow walk to a quick one and the puppy will come to adjust. The slow walk is always the more difficult for most puppies, as they are usually anxious to be on the move.

If you have no wall to walk against then things will be a little more difficult because the pup will tend to wander to his left. This means you need to give lateral jerks as well as bring the pup to your side. End the lesson when the pup is walking nicely beside you. Begin the lesson with a few sit commands (which he understands by now), so you're starting with success and praise. If your puppy is nervous on the leash, you should never drag him to your side as you may see so many other people do (who obviously didn't invest in a good book like you did!). If the pup sits down, call him to your side and give lots of praise. The pup must always come to you because he wants to. If he is dragged to your side he will see you doing the dragging—a big negative. When he races ahead he does not see you jerk the leash, so all he knows is that something restricted his movement and, once he was in a given position, you gave him lots of praise. This is using canine psychology to your advantage.

Always try to remember that if a dog must be disciplined, then try not to let him associate the discipline with you. This is not possible in all matters but, where it is, this is definitely to be preferred.

THE STAY COMMAND

This command follows from the sit. Face the puppy and say "Sit." Now step backwards, and as you do, say "Stay." Let the pup remain in the position for only a few seconds before calling him to you and giving lots of praise. Repeat this, but step further back. You do not need to shout at the puppy. Your pet is not deaf; in fact, his hearing is far better than yours. Speak just loudly enough for the pup to hear, yet use a firm voice. You can stretch the word to form a "sta-a-a-y." If the pup gets up and comes to you simply lift him up, place him back in the original position, and start again. As the pup comes to understand the command, you can move further and further back.

The next test is to walk away after placing the pup. This will mean your back is to him, which will tempt him to follow you. Keep an eye over your shoulder, and the minute the pup starts to move, spin around and, using a sterner voice, say either "Sit" or "Stay." If the pup has gotten quite close to you, then, again, return him to the original position.

As the weeks go by you can increase the length of time the pup is left in the stay position—but two to three minutes is quite long enough for a puppy. If your puppy drops into a lying position and is clearly more comfortable, there is nothing wrong with this. Likewise, your pup will want to face the direction in which you walked off. Some trainers will insist that the dog faces the direction he was placed in, regardless of whether you move off on his blind side. I have never believed in this sort of obedience because it has no practical benefit.

THE DOWN COMMAND

From the puppy's viewpoint, the down command can be one of the more difficult ones to accept. This is because the position is one taken up by a submissive dog in a wild pack situation. A timid dog will roll over—a natural gesture of submission. A bolder pup will want to get up, and might back off, not feeling he should have to submit to this command. He will feel that he is under attack from you and about to be punished—which is what would be the position in his natural environment. Once he comes to understand this is not the case, he will accept this unnatural position without any problem.

You may notice that some dogs will sit very quickly, but will respond to the down command more slowly—it is their way of saying that they will obey the command, but under protest!

There two ways to teach this command. One is, in my mind, more intimidating than the other, but it is up to you to decide which one works best for you. The first method is to stand in front of your puppy and bring him to the sit position, with his collar and leash on. Pass the leash under your left foot so that when you pull on it, the result is that the pup's neck is forced downwards. With your free left hand, push the pup's shoulders down while at the same time saying "Down." This is when a bold pup will instantly try to back off and wriggle in full protest. Hold the pup firmly by the shoulders so he stays in the position for a second or two, then tell him what a good dog he is and give him lots of praise. Repeat this only a few times in a lesson because otherwise the puppy will get bored and upset over this command. End with an easy command that brings back the pup's confidence.

The second method, and the one I prefer, is done as follows: Stand in front of the pup and then tell him to sit. Now kneel down, which is immediately far less intimidating to the puppy than to have you towering above him. Take each of his front legs and pull them forward, at the same time saying "Down." Release the legs and quickly apply light pressure on the shoulders with your left hand. Then, as quickly, say "Good boy" and give lots of fuss. Repeat two or three times only. The pup will learn over a few lessons. Remember, this is a very submissive act on the pup's behalf, so there is no need to rush matters.

RECALL TO HEEL COMMAND

When your puppy is coming to the heel position from an off-leash situation—such as if he has been running free—he should do this in the correct manner. He should pass behind you and take up his position and then sit. To teach this command, have the pup in front of you in the sit position with his collar and leash on. Hold the leash in your right hand. Give him the command to heel, and pat your left knee. As the pup starts to move forward, use your right hand to guide him behind you. If need be you can hold his collar and walk the dog around the back of you to the desired position. You will need to repeat this a few times until the dog understands what is wanted.

When he has done this a number of times, you can try it without the collar and leash. If the pup comes up toward your left side, then bring him to the sit position in front of you, hold his collar and walk him around the back of you. He will eventually understand and automatically pass around your back each time. If the dog is already behind you when you recall him, then he should automatically come to your left side, which you will be patting with your hand.

THE NO COMMAND

This is a command that must be obeyed every time without fail. There are no halfway stages, he must be 100-percent reliable. Most delinquent dogs have never been taught this command; included in these are the jumpers, the barkers, and the biters. Were your puppy to approach a poisonous snake or any other potential danger, the no command, coupled with the recall, could save his life. You do not need to give a specific lesson for this command because it will crop up time and again in day-to-day life.

If the puppy is chewing a slipper, you should approach the pup, take hold of the slipper, and say "No" in a stern voice. If he jumps onto the furniture, lift him off and say "No" and place him gently on the floor. You must be consistent in the use of the command and apply it every time he is doing something you do not want him to do.

YOUR HEALTHY DANDIE DINMONT

Dogs, like all other animals, are capable of contracting problems and diseases that, in most cases, are easily avoided by sound husbandry—meaning well-bred and well-cared-for animals are less prone to developing diseases and problems than are carelessly bred and neglected animals. Your knowledge of how to avoid problems is far more valuable than all of the books and advice on how to cure them. Respectively, the only person you should listen to about treatment is your vet. Veterinarians don't have all the answers, but at least they are trained to analyze and treat illnesses, and are aware of the full implications of treatments. This does not mean a few old remedies aren't good standbys when all else fails, but in most cases modern science provides the best treatments for disease.

Opposite: Veterinarians are trained to analyze and treat illnesses. Having complete trust in your chosen veterinarian is tantamount to the long life of your dog.

PHYSICAL EXAMS

Your puppy should receive regular physical examinations or check-ups. These come in two forms. One is obviously performed by your vet, and the other is a day-to-day procedure that should be done by you. Apart from the fact the exam will highlight any problem at an early stage, it is an excellent way of socializing the pup to being handled.

To do the physical exam yourself, start at the head and work your way around the body. You are looking for any sign of lesions, or any indication of parasites on the pup. The most common parasites are fleas and ticks.

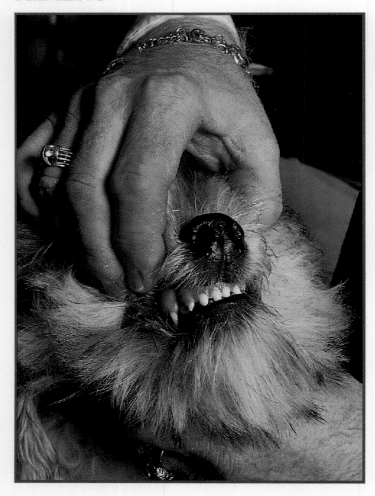

A thorough oral exam should be a part of your Dandie Dinmont's regular veterinary check-up.

HEALTHY TEETH AND GUMS

Chewing is instinctual. Puppies chew so that their teeth and jaws grow strong and healthy as they develop. As the permanent teeth begin to emerge, it is painful and annoying to the puppy, and puppy owners must recognize that their new charges need something safe upon which to chew. Unfortunately, once the puppy's permanent teeth have emerged and settled solidly into the jaw, the chewing instinct does not fade. Adult dogs instinctively need to clean their teeth, massage their gums, and exercise their jaws through chewing.

It is necessary for your dog to have clean teeth. You should take your dog to the veterinarian at least once a year to have his teeth cleaned and to have his mouth examined for any sign of oral disease. Although dogs do not get cavities in the same way humans do, dogs'

The Hercules® by Nylabone® has raised dental tips that help fight plaque on your Dandie Dinmont's teeth and gums.

teeth accumulate tartar, and more quickly than humans do! Veterinarians recommend brushing your dog's teeth daily. But who can find time to brush their dog's teeth daily? The accumulation of tartar and plaque on our dog's teeth when not removed can cause irritation and eventually erode the enamel and finally destroy the teeth. Advanced cases, while destroying the teeth, bring on gingivitis and periodontitis, two very serious conditions that can affect the dog's internal organs as well...to say nothing about bad breath!

Since everyone can't brush their dog's teeth daily or get to the veterinarian often enough for him to scale

Nylafloss® does wonders for your Dandie Dinmont's dental health by massaging his gums and literally flossing between his teeth, loosening plaque and tartar build-up. Unlike cotton tug toys, Nylafloss® won't rot or fray.

the dog's teeth, providing the dog with something safe to chew on will help maintain oral hygeine. Chew devices from Nylabone® keep dogs' teeth clean, but they also provide an excellent resource for entertainment and relief of doggie tensions. Nylabone® products give your dog something to do for an hour or two every day and during that hour or two, your dog will be taking an active part in keeping his teeth and gums healthy…without even realizing it! That's invaluable to your dog, and valuable to you!

Nylabone® provides fun bones, challenging bones, and *safe* bones. It is an owner's responsibility to recognize safe chew toys from dangerous ones. Your dog will chew and devour anything you give him. Dogs must not be permitted to chew on items that they can break. Pieces of broken objects can do internal damage to a dog, besides ripping the dog's mouth. Cheap plastic or rubber toys can cause stoppage in the intestines; such stoppages are operable only if caught immediately.

The most obvious choices, in this case, may be the worst choice. Natural beef bones were not designed for chewing and cannot take too much pressure from the sides. Due to the abrasive nature of these bones, they should be offered most sparingly. Knuckle bones, though once very popular for dogs, can be easily

Nylabone® is the only plastic dog bone made of 100% virgin nylon, specially processed to create a tough, durable, completely safe bone.

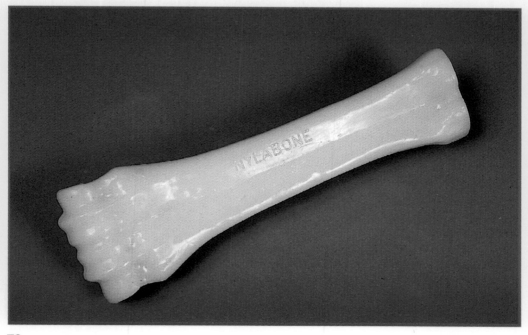

Chick-n-Cheez Chooz® are completely safe and nutritious health chews made from pure cheese protein, chicken, and fortified with vitamin E. They contain no salt, sugar, plastic, or preservatives and less than 1% fat.

chewed up and eaten by dogs. At the very least, digestion is interrupted; at worst, the dog can choke or suffer from intestinal blockage.

When a dog chews hard on a Nylabone®, little bristle-like projections appear on the surface of the bone. These help to clean the dog's teeth and add to the gum-massaging. Given the chemistry of the nylon, the bristle can pass through the dog's intestinal tract without effect. Since nylon is inert, no micro-organism can grow on it, and it can be washed in soap and water or sterilized in boiling water or in an autoclave.

For the sake of your dog, his teeth and your own peace of mind, provide your dog with Nylabones®. They have 100 variations from which to choose.

FIGHTING FLEAS

Fleas are very mobile and may be red, black, or brown in color. The adults suck the blood of the host, while the larvae feed on the feces of the adults, which is rich in blood. Flea "dirt" may be seen on the pup as very tiny clusters of blackish specks that look like freshly ground pepper. The eggs of fleas may be laid on the puppy, though they are more commonly laid off the host in a favorable place, such as the bedding. They normally hatch in 4 to 21 days, depending on the temperature, but they can survive for up to 18 months if temperature conditions are not favorable. The larvae are maggot-like and molt a couple of times before forming pupae, which can survive long periods until the temperature, or the vibration of a nearby host, causes them to emerge and jump on a host.

There are a number of effective treatments available, and you should discuss them with your veterinarian, then follow all instructions for the one you choose. Any treatment will involve a product for your puppy or dog and one for the environment, and will require diligence on your part to treat all areas and thoroughly clean your home and yard until the infestation is eradicated.

THE TROUBLE WITH TICKS

Ticks are arthropods of the spider family, which means they have eight legs (though the larvae have six). They bury their headparts into the host and gorge on its blood. They are easily seen as small grain-like creatures sticking out from the skin. They are often picked up when dogs play in fields, but may also arrive in your yard via wild animals—even birds—or stray cats and dogs. Some ticks are species-specific, others are more adaptable and will host on many species.

The cat flea is the most common flea of dogs. It starts feeding soon after it makes contact with the dog.

The deer tick is the most common carrier of Lyme disease. Photo courtesy of Virbac Laboratories, Inc., Fort Worth, Texas.

The most troublesome type of tick is the deer tick, which spreads the deadly Lyme disease that can cripple a dog (or a person). Deer ticks are tiny and very hard to detect. Often, by the time they're big enough to notice, they've been feeding on the dog for a few days—long enough to do their damage. Lyme disease was named for the area of the United States in which it was first detected—Lyme, Connecticut—but has now been diagnosed in almost all parts of the U.S. Your veterinarian can advise you of the danger to your dog(s) in your area, and may suggest your dog be vaccinated for Lyme. Always go over your dog with a fine-toothed flea comb when you come in from walking through any area that may harbor deer ticks, and if your dog is acting unusually sluggish or sore, seek veterinary advice.

Attempts to pull a tick free will invariably leave the headpart in the pup, where it will die and cause an infected wound or abscess. The best way to remove ticks is to dab a strong saline solution, iodine, or alcohol on them. This will numb them, causing them to loosen their hold, at which time they can be removed with forceps. The wound can then be cleaned and covered with an antiseptic ointment. If ticks are common in your area, consult with your vet for a suitable pesticide to be used in kennels, on bedding, and on the puppy or dog.

INSECTS AND OTHER OUTDOOR DANGERS

There are many biting insects, such as mosquitoes, that can cause discomfort to a puppy. Many diseases are transmitted by the males of these species.

A pup can easily get a grass seed or thorn lodged between his pads or in the folds of his ears. These may go unnoticed until an abscess forms.

This is where your daily check of the puppy or dog will do a world of good. If your puppy has been playing in long grass or places where there may be thorns, pine needles, wild animals, or parasites, the check-up is a wise precaution.

SKIN DISORDERS

Apart from problems associated with lesions created by biting pests, a puppy may fall foul to a number of other skin disorders. Examples are ringworm, mange, and eczema. Ringworm is not caused by a worm, but is a fungal infection. It manifests itself as a sore-looking bald circle. If your puppy should have any form of bald patches, let your veterinarian check him over; a microscopic examination can confirm the condition. Many old remedies for ringworm exist, such as iodine, carbolic acid, formalin, and other tinctures, but modern drugs are superior.

After he plays outdoors, check your Dandie's coat thoroughly for parasites such as fleas and ticks.

Fungal infections can be very difficult to treat, and even more difficult to eradicate, because of the spores. These can withstand most treatments, other than burning, which is the best thing to do with bedding once the condition has been confirmed.

Mange is a general term that can be applied to many skin conditions where the hair falls out and a flaky crust develops and falls away.

Often, dogs will scratch themselves, and this invariably is worse than the original condition, for it opens lesions that are then subject to viral, fungal, or parasitic attack. The cause of the problem can be various species of mites. These either live on skin debris and the hair follicles, which they destroy, or they bury themselves just beneath the skin and feed on the tissue. Applying general remedies from pet stores is not recommended because it is essential to identify the type of mange before a specific treatment is effective.

Eczema is another non-specific term applied to many skin disorders. The condition can be brought about in many ways. Sunburn, chemicals, allergies to foods, drugs, pollens, and even stress can all produce a deterioration of the skin and coat. Given the range of causal factors, treatment can be difficult because the problem is one of identification. It is a case of taking each possibility at a time and trying to correctly diagnose the matter. If the cause is of a dietary nature then you must remove one item at a time in order to find out if the dog is allergic to a given food. It could, of course, be the lack of a nutrient that is the problem, so if the condition persists, you should consult your veterinarian.

INTERNAL DISORDERS

It cannot be overstressed that it is very foolish to attempt to diagnose an internal disorder without the advice of a veterinarian. Take a relatively common problem such as diarrhea. It might be caused by nothing more serious than the puppy hogging a lot of food or eating something that it has never previously eaten. Conversely, it could be the first indication of a potentially fatal disease. It's up to your veterinarian to make the correct diagnosis.

The following symptoms, especially if they accompany each other or are progressively added to earlier symptoms, mean you should visit the veterinarian right away:

77

Continual vomiting. All dogs vomit from time to time and this is not necessarily a sign of illness. They will eat grass to induce vomiting. It is a natural cleansing process common to many carnivores. However, continued vomiting is a clear sign of a problem. It may be a blockage in the pup's intestinal tract, it may be induced by worms, or it could be due to any number of diseases.

Diarrhea. This, too, may be nothing more than a temporary condition due to many factors. Even a change of home can induce diarrhea, because this often stresses the pup, and invariably there is some change in the diet. If it persists more than 48 hours then something is amiss. If blood is seen in the feces, waste no time at all in taking the dog to the vet.

Running eyes and/or nose. A pup might have a chill and this will cause the eyes and nose to weep. Again, this should quickly clear up if the puppy is placed in a warm environment and away from any drafts. If it does not, and especially if a mucous discharge is seen, then the pup has an illness that must be diagnosed.

Coughing. Prolonged coughing is a sign of a problem, usually of a respiratory nature.

Wheezing. If the pup has difficulty breathing and makes a wheezing sound when breathing, then something is wrong.

Cries when attempting to defecate or urinate. This might only be a minor problem due to the hard state of the feces, but it could be more serious, especially if the pup cries when urinating.

Cries when touched. Obviously, if you do not handle a puppy with care he might yelp. However, if he cries even when lifted gently, then he has an internal problem that becomes apparent when pressure is applied to a given area of the body. Clearly, this must be diagnosed.

Refuses food. Generally, puppies and dogs are greedy creatures when it comes to feeding time. Some might be more fussy, but none should refuse more than one meal. If they go for a number of hours without showing any interest in their food, then something is not as it should be.

General listlessness. All puppies have their off days when they do not seem their usual cheeky, mischievous selves. If this condition persists for more than two days then there is little doubt of a problem. They may not show any of the signs listed, other than perhaps a reduced interest in their food. There are many diseases that can develop internally without displaying obvious clinical signs. Blood, fecal, and other tests are needed in order to identify the disorder before it reaches an advanced state that may not be treatable.

WORMS

There are many species of worms, and a number of these live in the tissues of dogs and most other animals. Many create no problem at all, so you are not even aware they exist. Others can be tolerated in small levels, but become a major problem if they number more than a few. The most common types seen in dogs are roundworms and tapeworms. While roundworms are the greater problem, tapeworms require an intermediate host so are more easily eradicated.

Roundworms are spaghetti-like worms that cause a pot-bellied appearance and dull coat, along with more severe symptoms, such as diarrhea and vomiting. Photo courtesy of Merck AgVet.

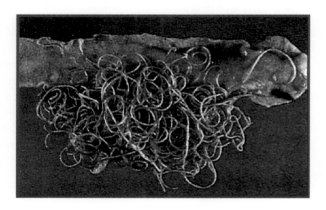

Roundworms of the species *Toxocara canis* infest the dog. They may grow to a length of 8 inches (20 cm) and look like strings of spaghetti. The worms feed on the digesting food in the pup's intestines. In chronic cases the puppy will become pot-bellied, have diarrhea, and will vomit. Eventually, he will stop eating, having passed through the stage when he always seems hungry. The worms lay eggs in the puppy and these pass out in his feces. They are then either ingested by the pup, or they are eaten by mice, rats, or beetles. These may then be eaten by the puppy and the life cycle is complete.

Larval worms can migrate to the womb of a pregnant bitch, or to her mammary glands, and this is how they pass to the puppy. The pregnant bitch can be wormed, which will help. The pups can, and should,

Whipworms are hard to find unless you strain your dog's feces, and this is best left to a veterinarian. Pictured here are adult whipworms.

be wormed when they are about two weeks old. Repeat worming every 10 to 14 days and the parasites should be removed. Worms can be extremely dangerous to young puppies, so you should be sure the pup is wormed as a matter of routine.

Tapeworms can be seen as tiny rice-like eggs sticking to the puppy's or dog's anus. They are less destructive, but still undesirable. The eggs are eaten by mice, fleas, rabbits, and other animals that serve as intermediate hosts. They develop into a larval stage and the host must be eaten by the dog in order to complete the chain. Your vet will supply a suitable remedy if tapeworms are seen or suspected. There are other worms, such as hookworms and whipworms, that are also blood suckers. They will make a pup anemic, and blood might be seen in the feces, which can be examined by the vet to confirm their presence. Cleanliness in all matters is the best preventative measure for all worms.

Heartworm infestation in dogs is passed by mosquitoes but can be prevented by a monthly (or daily) treatment that is given orally. Talk to your vet about the risk of heartworm in your area.

BLOAT (GASTRIC DILATATION)

This condition has proved fatal in many dogs, especially large and deep-chested breeds, such as the Weimaraner and the Great Dane. However, any dog can get bloat. It is caused by swallowing air during exercise, food/water gulping or another strenuous task. As many believe, it is not the result of flatulence. The stomach of an affected dog twists, disallowing food and blood flow and resulting in harmful toxins being released into the bloodstream. Death can easily follow if the condition goes undetected.

The best preventative measure is not to feed large meals or exercise your puppy or dog immediately after he has eaten. Veterinarians recommend feeding three smaller meals per day in an elevated feeding rack, adding water to dry food to prevent gulping, and not offering water during mealtimes.

VACCINATIONS

Every puppy, purebred or mixed breed, should be vaccinated against the major canine diseases. These are distemper, leptospirosis, hepatitis, and canine parvovirus. Your puppy may have received a temporary vaccination against distemper before you purchased him, but be sure to ask the breeder to be sure.

The age at which vaccinations are given can vary, but will usually be when the pup is 8 to 12 weeks old. By this time any protection given to the pup by antibodies received from his mother via her initial milk feeds will be losing their strength.

Rely on your veterinarian for the most effectual vaccination schedule for your Dandie Dinmont puppy.

The puppy's immune system works on the basis that the white blood cells engulf and render harmless

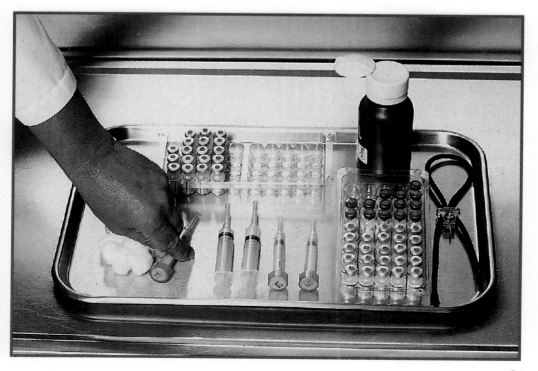

attacking bacteria. However, they must first recognize a potential enemy.

Vaccines are either dead bacteria or they are live, but in very small doses. Either type prompts the pup's defense system to attack them. When a large attack then comes (if it does), the immune system recognizes it and massive numbers of lymphocytes (white blood corpuscles) are mobilized to counter the attack. However, the ability of the cells to recognize these dangerous viruses can diminish over a period of time. It is therefore useful to provide annual reminders about the nature of the enemy. This is done by means of booster injections that keep the immune system on its alert. Immunization is not 100-percent guaranteed to be successful, but is very close. Certainly it is better than giving the puppy no protection.

Dogs are subject to other viral attacks, and if these are of a high-risk factor in your area, then your vet will suggest you have the puppy vaccinated against these as well.

Your puppy or dog should also be vaccinated against the deadly rabies virus. In fact, in many places it is illegal for your dog not to be vaccinated. This is to protect your dog, your family, and the rest of the animal population from this deadly virus that infects the nervous system and causes dementia and death.

ACCIDENTS

All puppies will get their share of bumps and bruises due to the rather energetic way they play. These will usually heal themselves over a few days. Small cuts should be bathed with a suitable disinfectant and then smeared with an antiseptic ointment. If a cut looks more serious, then stem the flow of blood with a towel or makeshift tourniquet and rush the pup to the veterinarian. Never apply so much pressure to the wound that it might restrict the flow of blood to the limb.

In the case of burns you should apply cold water or an ice pack to the surface. If the burn was due to a chemical, then this must be washed away with copious amounts of water. Apply petroleum jelly, or any vegetable oil, to the burn. Trim away the hair if need be. Wrap the dog in a blanket and rush him to the vet. The pup may go into shock, depending on the severity of the burn, and this will result in a lowered blood pressure, which is dangerous and the reason the pup must receive immediate veterinary attention.

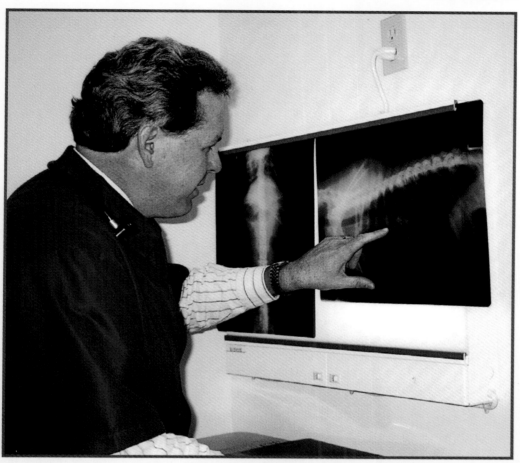

It is a good idea to x-ray the chest and abdomen on any dog hit by a car.

If a broken limb is suspected then try to keep the animal as still as possible. Wrap your pup or dog in a blanket to restrict movement and get him to the veterinarian as soon as possible. Do not move the dog's head so it is tilting backward, as this might result in blood entering the lungs.

Do not let your pup jump up and down from heights, as this can cause considerable shock to the joints. Like all youngsters, puppies do not know when enough is enough, so you must do all their thinking for them.

Provided you apply strict hygiene to all aspects of raising your puppy, and you make daily checks on his physical state, you have done as much as you can to safeguard him during his most vulnerable period. Routine visits to your veterinarian are also recommended, especially while the puppy is under one year of age. The vet may notice something that did not seem important to you.

CONGENITAL AND ACQUIRED DISORDERS

by Judy Iby, RVT

Veterinarians and breeders now recognize that many of the disease processes and faults in dogs, as well as in human beings, have a genetic predisposition. These faults are found not only in the purebred dog but in the mixed breed as well. Likely these diseases have been present for decades but more recently are being identified and attributed to inheritance. Fortunately many of these problems are not life threatening or even debilitating. Many of these disorders have a low incidence. It is true that some breeds and some bloodlines within a breed have a higher frequency than others. It is always wise to discuss this subject with breeders of your breed.

Presently very few of the hundreds of disorders can be identified through genetic testing. Hopefully with today's technology and the desire to improve our breeding stock, genetic testing will become more readily available. In the meantime the reputable breeder does the recommended testing for his breed. The American Kennel Club is encouraging OFA (Orthopedic Foundation for Animals) hip and elbow certification and CERF (Canine Eye Registration Foundation) certifications and is listing them on AKC registrations and pedigrees. This is a step forward for the AKC in encouraging better breeding. They also founded a Canine Health Foundation to aid in the research of diseases in the purebred dog.

Opposite: The responsible Dandie Dinmont breeder, understanding the potential problems within the breed, strives to produce healthy puppies and contribute to the betterment of the breed.

BONES AND JOINTS

Hip Dysplasia

Canine hip dysplasia has been confirmed in 79 breeds. It is the malformation of the hip joint's ball and socket, with clinical signs from none to severe hip lameness. It may appear as early as five months. The incidence is

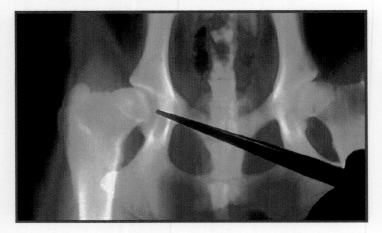

Radiograph of a dog with hip dysplasia. Note the flattened femoral head at the marker. Photo courtesy of Toronto Academy of Veterinary Medicine, Toronto, Canada.

reduced within a bloodline by breeding normal to normal, generation after generation. Upon submitting normal pelvic radiographs, the OFA will issue a certification number.

Elbow Dysplasia

Elbow dysplasia results from abnormal development of the ulna, one of the bones of the upper arm. During bone growth, a small area of bone (the anconeal process) fails to fuse with the rest of the bone. This results in an unstable elbow joint and lameness, which is aggravated by exercise. OFA certifies free of this disorder.

Patellar Luxation

This condition can be medial or lateral. Breeders call patellar luxations "slips" for "slipped kneecaps." OFA offers a registry for this disorder. Patellar luxations may or may not cause problems.

Intervertebral Disk Disease (IVD)

IVD is a condition in which a disk(s), the cushion between each vertebrae of the spine, tears and the gel-like material leaks out and presses on the spinal cord. The degeneration is progressive, starting as early as two to nine months, but usually the neurological symptoms are not apparent until three to six years of age. Symptoms include pain, paresis (weariness), incoordination, and paralysis. IVD is a medical emergency. If you are unable to get professional care immediately, then confine your dog to a crate or small area until he can be seen.

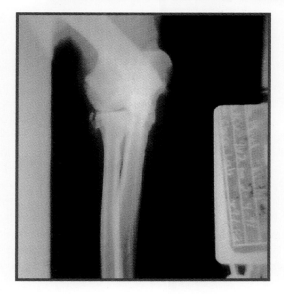

Fragmented coronoid process of the elbow, a manifestation of elbow dysplasia. Photo courtesy of Jack Henry.

Spondylitis

Usually seen in middle to old-age dogs and potentially quite serious in the latter, spondylitis is inflammation of the vertebral joints and degeneration of intervertebral disks resulting in bony spur-like outgrowths that may fuse.

CARDIOVASCULAR AND LYMPHATIC SYSTEMS

Dilated Cardiomyopathy

Prevalent in several breeds, this is a disease in which the heart muscle is damaged or destroyed to the point that it cannot pump blood properly through the body resulting in signs of heart failure. Diagnosis is confirmed by cardiac ultrasound.

Lymphosarcoma

This condition can occur in young dogs but usually appears in dogs over the age of five years. Symptoms include fever, weight loss, anorexia, painless enlargement of the lymph nodes, and nonspecific signs of illness. It is the most common type of cancer found in dogs. Chemotherapy treatment will prolong the dog's life but will not cure the disease at this time.

BLOOD

Von Willebrand's Disease

VWD has been confirmed in over 50 breeds and is

a manageable disease. It is characterized by moderate to severe bleeding, corrected by blood transfusions from normal dogs and frequently seen with hypothyroidism. When levels are low, a pre-surgical blood transfusion may be necessary. Many breeders screen their breeding stock for vWD.

Immune-Mediated Blood Disease

Immune-mediated diseases affect the red blood cells and platelets. They are called autoimmune hemolytic anemia or immune-mediated anemia when red blood cells are affected, and autoimmune thrombocytopenic purpura, idiopathic thrombocytopenic purpura, and immune-mediated thrombocytopenia when platelets are involved. The disease may appear acutely. Symptoms include jaundice (yellow color) of the gums and eyes and dark brown or dark red urine. Symptoms of platelet disease include pinpoint bruises or hemorrhages in the skin, gums and eye membranes; nosebleeds; bleeding from the GI tract or into the urine. Any of these symptoms constitutes an emergency!

DIGESTIVE SYSTEM AND ORAL CAVITY

Colitis

This disorder has no known cause and appears with some frequency in certain breeds. It is characterized by an intermittent bloody stool, with or without diarrhea.

Chronic Hepatitis

This is the result of liver failure occuring at relatively young ages. In many cases clinical signs are apparent for less than two weeks. They include anorexia, lethargy, vomiting, depression, diarrhea, trembling or shaking, excess thirst and urination, weight loss, and dark bloody stool. Early diagnosis and treatment promise the best chance for survival.

Copper Toxicity

Copper toxicity occurs when excessive copper is concentrated in the liver. In 1995 there was a breakthrough when the DNA marker was identified in one of the afflicted breeds. Therefore carriers will be identified in the future.

ENDOCRINE SYSTEM

Hypothyroidism

Over 50 breeds have been diagnosed with hypothyroidism. It is the number-one endocrine disorder in the dog and is the result of an underactive thyroid gland. Conscientious breeders are screening their dogs if the disease is common to their breed or bloodline. The critical years for the decline of thyroid function are usually between three and eight, although it can appear at an older age. A simple blood test can diagnose or rule out this disorder. It is easily and inexpensively treated by giving thyroid replacement therapy daily. Untreated hypothyroidism can be devastating to your dog.

Addison's Disease

Primary adrenal insufficiency is caused by damage to the adrenal cortex, and secondary adrenocortical insufficiency is the result of insufficient production of the hormone ACTH by the pituitary gland. Symptoms may include depression, anorexia, a weak femoral pulse, vomiting or diarrhea, weakness, dehydration, and occasionally bradycardia.

Cushing's Disease

Hyperadrenocorticism is the over-production of steroid hormone. Dogs on steroid therapy may show Cushing-like symptoms. Some of the symptoms are excess thirst and urination, hair loss, and an enlarged, pendulous, or flaccid abdomen.

EYES

Cataracts

Breeders should screen their breeding stock for this disorder. A cataract is defined as any opacity of the lens or its capsule. It may progress and produce blindness or it may remain small and cause no clinical impairment of vision. Unfortunately some inherited cataracts appear later in life after the dog has already been bred.

Lens Luxation

This condition results when the lens of the eye is not in normal position, and may result in secondary glaucoma.

CONGENITAL DISORDERS

Glaucoma

Primary glaucoma is caused by increased intraocular pressure due to inadequate aqueous drainage and is not associated with other intraocular diseases. It may initially be in one eye. Secondary glaucoma is caused by increased intraocular pressure brought on by another ocular disease, tumor, or inflammation.

Keratoconjunctivitis Sicca

"Dry eye" (the decrease in production of tears) may be the result of a congenital or inherited deficiency of the aqueous layer, a lack of the proper nervous stimulation of the tearing system, a traumatic incident, or drugs, including topical anesthetics (such as

An immature cataract is evident in this dilated pupil. The central white area and cloudy areas at 4:00, 6:00 and 8:00 represent the cataract. Photo courtesy of Dr. Kerry L. Ketring.

atropine, and antibiotics containing sulfadiazine, phenazopyridine or salicyla-sulfapyridine). There seems to be an increased incidence of "dry eye" after "cherry eye" removal.

Progressive Retinal Atrophy (PRA)

This is the progressive loss of vision, first at night, followed by total blindness. It is inherited in many breeds.

Distichiasis

Distichiasis results from extra rows of eyelashes growing out of the meibomian gland ducts. This condition may cause tearing, but tearing may be the result of some other problem that needs to be investigated.

Entropion

Entropion is the inward rolling of the eyelid, usually lower lid, which can cause inflammation and may need surgical correction.

Ectropion

Ectropion is the outward rolling of the eyelid, usually lower lid, and may need surgical correction.

Hypertrophy of the Nictitans Gland

"Cherry eye" is the increase in size of the gland resulting in eversion of the third eyelid and is usually bilateral. Onset frequently occurs during stressful periods such as teething.

NEUROMUSCULAR SYSTEM

Epilepsy

Epilepsy is a disorder in which the electrical brain activity "short circuits," resulting in a seizure. Numerous breeds and mixed breeds are subject to idiopathic epilepsy (no explainable reason). Seizures usually begin between six months and five years of age. Don't panic. Your primary concern should be to keep your dog from hurting himself by falling down the stairs or falling off furniture and/or banging his head. Dogs don't swallow their tongues. If the seizure lasts longer than ten minutes, you should contact your veterinarian. Seizures can be caused by many conditions, such as poisoning and birth injuries, brain infections, trauma or tumors, liver disease, distemper, and low blood sugar or calcium. There are all types of seizures from generalized (the dog will be shaking and paddling/kicking his feet) to standing and staring out in space, etc.

UROGENITAL

Cryptorchidism

This is a condition in which either one or both of the testes fail to descend into the scrotum. There should not be a problem if the dog is neutered early, before two to three years of age. Otherwise, the undescended testicle could turn cancerous.

PET OWNERS & BLOOD PRESSURE

Over the past few years, several scientific studies have documented many health benefits of having pets in our lives. At the State University of New York at Buffalo, for example, Dr. Karen Allen and her colleagues have focused on how physical reactions to psychological stress are influenced by the presence of pets. One such study compared the effect of pets with that of a person's close friend and reported pets to be dramatically better than friends at providing unconditional support. Blood pressure was monitored throughout the study, and, on average, the blood pressure of people under stress who were *with* their pets was 112/75, as compared to 140/95 when they were with the self-selected friends. Heart rate differences were also significantly lower when participants were with their pets. A follow-up study included married couples and looked at the stress-reducing effect of pets versus *spouses*, and found, once again, that pets were dramatically more successful than other people in reducing cardiovascular reactions to stress. An interesting discover made in this study was that when the spouse and pet were *both* present, heart rate and blood pressure came down dramatically; that is, the presence of the pet appeared to cancel out some of the anxiety produced by the presence of the spouse.

Other work by the same researchers has looked at the role of pets in moderating age-related increases in blood pressure. In a study that followed 100 women (half in their 20s and half in their 70s) over six months, it was found that elderly women with few social contacts and *no* pets had blood pressures that were significantly higher (averages of 145/95 compared to 120/80) than elderly women with their beloved pets but few *human* contacts. In other words, elderly women with pets, but no friends, had blood pressures that closely reflected the blood pressures of young women.

This series of studies demonstrates that pets can play an important role in how we handle everyday stress, and shows that biological aging cannot be fully understood without a consideration of the social factors in our lives.

More than best friends or even spouses, pets have a natural calming effect on their humans.

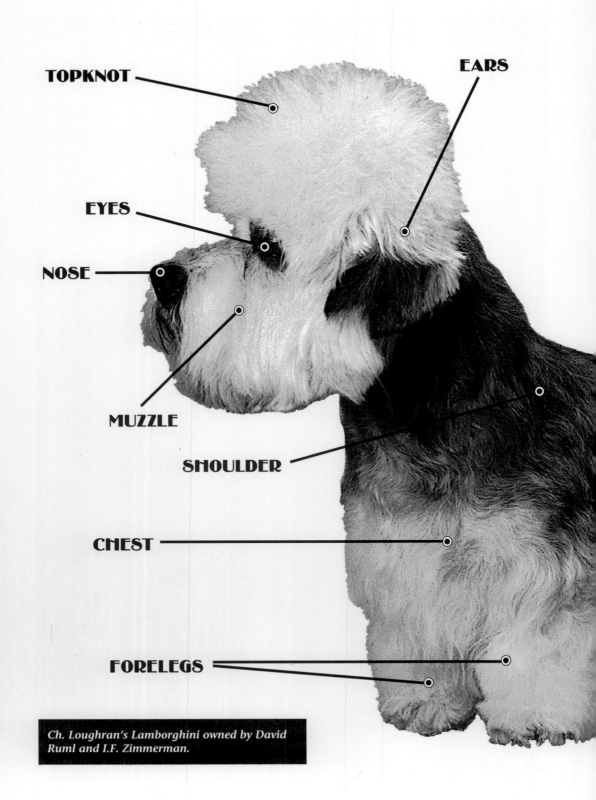

TOPKNOT

EARS

EYES

NOSE

MUZZLE

SHOULDER

CHEST

FORELEGS

Ch. Loughran's Lamborghini owned by David Ruml and I.F. Zimmerman.